Lookout!

Most prison[illegible] cold, bare floo[illegible] They only had water to eat a[illegible] them, disease tha[illegible] spre[illegible] prisoner to another often did!

There was a prisoner called Ned
Who dined before going to bed
On spiders and rats
Stale bread and stray cats
And when he woke up he was dead

The word [d]ungeon comes [f]rom donjon – [t]he French [w]ord for [k]eep.

Not all castles [illegible]s. [illegible] had [illegible]rd [illegible] [w]here prison[illegible] could be locked up overnight. Look out for guard rooms, dungeons and oubliettes. Find out what you score on page 13.

Handsome ransoms!

In times of trouble or war, important men and women were sometimes held prisoner for years!

Powerful prisoners such as foreign kings, lords and knights were valuable. They were usually treated well because they could be exchanged for huge sums of money (called a ransom). Sometimes important prisoners were exchanged for other things, such as the keys to a castle. If the keys weren't handed over, the prisoner was executed!

Lookout!

Sometimes prisoners left their mark on the prison walls – perhaps so they wouldn't be forgotten! Look out for names, pictures, or messages carved into walls. Find out what you score on page 13.

A prisoner carved this picture on the wall of Carlisle Castle, Cumbria.

HAND OVER YOUR SWEETS OR THE BUNNY GETS IT!

when you get home. . .

. . . make a RANSOM NOTE. Write your note on white writing paper. Soak two tea bags in half a cup of warm water. Lay the ransom note on newspaper. Wipe the teabags over the note staining it brown. Turn it over and stain the other side. Leave to dry then wipe over the edges to make them darker brown. Leave to dry. Roll it up into a scroll and tie with a red ribbon.

Terrible punishments

A lord usually settled arguments and dealt with small crimes in his castle. The king dealt with serious crimes in his own law courts.

n the Middle Ages, all punishment was ·ry rough. People ere put in prison for ›aching, begging or aking fake money. ·unks were whipped. aders who sold ulty goods were put in the stocks or pillory ıd pelted with rubbish. Robbers and urderers were hanged or burnt to death.

Lords or ladies to be punished by death could choose to be beheaded with an axe or a sword.

Lookout!

ı the Middle Ages, lords dealt with crimes in the Great Iall in the castle keep. So look out for a Great Hall in a astle. You might find stocks or a pillory in your local ıuseum. Find out what you score on page 13.

Traitor!

If people plot against their king, queen or country they are called a traitor. Traitors were punished by death.

Traitors were punished with the most horrible death of all. The lucky ones were beheaded. Their heads were stuck on poles and shown where everyone could see them. Others were burnt alive or hung, drawn and quartered. This means that after they were hung, their insides were taken out like a chicken, and their bodies cut into four pieces!

Who was the world's first underwater spy?

James Pond!

Micklega York. Traitors' heads we stuck on of the gateway.

Guy Fawkes was a traitor. On November 5 1605, he was caught trying to blow up James I and Parliament with gunpowder. It was called the Gunpowder Plot. Guy was caught and tortured. Then he was hung, drawn and quartered. Nearly 400 years later, we still remember Guy Fawkes on November 5 with bonfires and fireworks.

Lookout!

Traitors were often imprisoned in the Tower of London. In the Middle Ages, they entered the Tower through Traitors' Gate. So look out for Traitors' Gate at the Tower of London. In other parts of the country look out for castle gates or city gateways. Find out what you score on page 13.

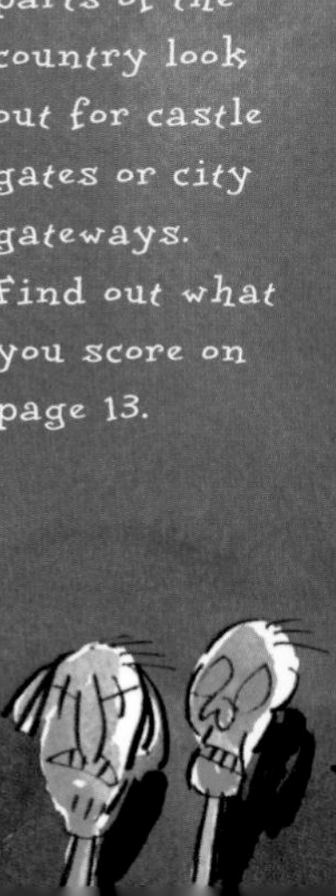

Famous prisoners

Over time, many famous prisoners have been locked up in castle prisons.

The Tower of London holds the record for the greatest number of famous prisoners. Anne Boleyn and Catherine Howard, two of Henry VIII's six wives, were imprisoned there and beheaded nearby. Guy Fawkes was tortured in the Tower. And two young princes are said to have been murdered there in 1483.

The Tower of London.

In 1327 Edward II was mprisoned in Berkeley Castle, n Gloucestershire. It is said lead animals were thrown into pit below his cell. His jailers oped that disease and the orrible smell might kill him. dward survived, but he was nurdered later!

In 1244 a /elsh prince called ruffydd ap Llewelyn as a prisoner in the ower of London. He tied neets together and wered himself out of a indow. But the sheets ame apart and he fell to is death.

Lookout!

There are hundreds of castles all over the country. Did one near you have a famous prisoner? Find out what you score on page 13.

Sneaky escapes

When people were put in prison they tried to escape as quickly as they could!

In the 1100s King Stephen and Empress Matilda were fighting over who should rule England. Stephen attacked Oxford Castle where Matilda was hiding. She had to escape! It was winter and snowing outside, so she put on a white dress. Then she lowered herself down a rope and sneaked over the frozen River Thames. But if anyone had seen her, they would have mistaken her for a ghost!

There were two skeletons locked up in the castle dungeon. What did one say to the other?

If we had the guts we'd get out of here!

. . . try this special ESCAPE KNOT called a bowline. Could it be used to escape from a prison tower? Tie it round a teddy's middle and lower it from a table!

In 1647 King Charles I ıs a prisoner in ‚risbrooke Castle on e Isle of Wight. His ends planned an cape. The King would squeeze through e bars of a window, lower himself down rope and escape on horseback. But ıarles forgot to check whether he could t through the bars and got stuck!

Lookout!

Look out for spiral stairs and dark passages in castles where people might have tried to escape, or hide. Find out what you score on page 13.

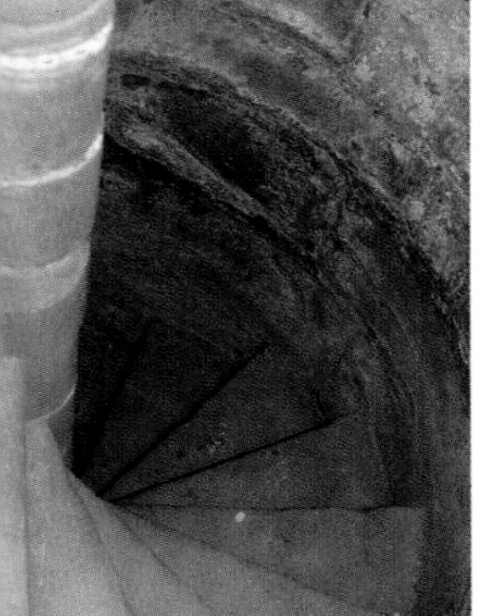

Spiral stairs, Warwick Castle, Warwickshire. Imagine creeping down these stairs and sneaking past the guard in the dark!

How to use the stickers

First find what you've got to look out for under this sign **Lookout!** Then peel off a sticker with the right number of points and stick it in the blank circle.

Score 20 for an oubliette

Score 20 for a dungeon

Score 10 for a guard room

Score 20 for a prisoner's mark

Score 10 for a Great Hall

Score 15 for the stocks or a pillory

Score 20 for Traitor's Gate

Score 5 for a castle gate or a city gateway

Score 10 for a castle which had a famous prisoner

Score 5 for spiral stairs

Score 5 for a dark passage